JUST JOKES

Adult Golf Humor

"If we couldn't laugh, we would all go insane." - *Robert Frost*

TEAM GOLFWELL

Adults Only

All images are from Creative Commons.

All jokes are fictitious.

Contents

Adult Golf Jokes

Joe and the rest of his foursome had a late dinner after their regular Saturday late afternoon round. They wound up binge drinking way too much after finishing dinner. Joe staggered home late at night.

He took off his shoes as he came through the door not wanting to wake his wife.

He tiptoed quietly up the stairs to the bedroom but tripped over the first step, twisted, and fell on his ass.

He forgot about the half-pint of whiskey in his back pocket that partially broke as he landed. Some of the glass cut his butt and the whiskey soaked the stairs with what was left in the bottle. He fought not to scream out loud and not disturb his sleeping wife.

He stumbled over to the hall mirror, took off his pants, and saw he had several bleeding cuts on his butt from the broken bottle.

He luckily stopped the bleeding then found a box of Band-Aids in the downstair bathroom and went back to the hall mirror and put them on his butt as best as he could over areas that were cut. He carefully put the Band-Aids back and climbed the stairs to the bedroom.

The next morning, he woke early with a massive headache not to mention a very painful butt. When he opened his eyes, his wife was staring at him from across the room.

“Drunk again, weren’t you?”

Trying to hide what happened, he replied, “What makes you think that honey?”

“Well, let’s see, maybe it was the open front door? Or the broken glass at the bottom of the stairs? Or the trail of blood throughout the house? Or your bloodshot eyes?”

He silently kept listening to her.

"But what convinced me the most was all those Band-Aids stuck on the hall mirror!"

Jim and Joanna are having a blind date at a well-known Italian restaurant. Jim ordered the Lasagne and Joanna ordered spaghetti. Both dishes were difficult to eat without staining clothes.

A drop of tomato sauce landed on Joanna's beautiful white top.

"Oh my, look at that! I'm a pig," Joanna said.

Jim nodded his agreement as he ate his lasagne. "You also have a drop of tomato sauce on your top!"

Jim isn't out of the hospital yet, and it may be a few weeks before he gets out.

What goes with a fried egg in the bunker?

A club sand wedge!

Pete had a late afternoon round of golf and one thing led to another and he wound up bar-hopping with the other three single guys.

It was 11 pm and Pete could hardly walk and sat at the bar with his head hung down wondering how the hell he was going to explain all this to his wife who he loved very much.

One of his friends noticed Pete in deep despair, and put his arm around his shoulder and said, “Worried about the other half?”

"Yes, I don't know have any idea what to tell her."

"Listen, Pete, when I mess up and come home to my girlfriend there is one thing that works every time."

"Nothing is going to work," Pete mumbled.

"Now don't give up. Here's what I do. When I come home, I make as little noise as possible and tiptoe to the bedroom. Before she can say anything, I start pleasing her with oral sex. Now, mind you, I don't stop for anything. I just keep at it for a good 30 minutes. By the time I'm done, it's all good."

So, Pete went home and took his shoes off before going into the house. He tiptoed up the stairs as quietly as he could. He went into the bedroom and lifted the sheet and began oral sex just as his friend suggested. She tried to push him away, but Pete kept at it for 30 minutes and didn't stop.

Finally, he finished, got up, and went to use the downstairs bathroom since he didn't want to wake his wife who apparently fell asleep from exhaustion.

As he came down the stairs and walked into the downstairs bathroom, he saw his wife standing at the sink.

"What the hell?" Pete said.

"Quiet, you'll wake my mother. Oh, I forgot to tell you, honey, my mother is staying for a visit and I let her use our bedroom."

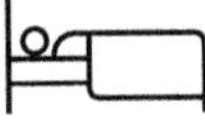

One for the 19th hole. John was shy and very bashful and had difficulty talking to girls. He hardly ever had a date and the few times he did, he usually said the wrong thing. He wanted a girlfriend more than anything.

So, he asked his best friend Bill to help him at a singles bar after they got done golfing late on a Saturday to have a beer or two and hopefully meet a girl.

Bill was an excellent ladies' man with good looks and a lot of experience. John was hoping he would help him find a girl and he could have a partner and enjoy all the good things a relationship would bring as well as have sex for the first time.

While they were at the bar John noticed a girl was eyeballing at him. He checked if anyone was seated behind him but there wasn't anyone there. Then he came to realize this beautiful girl was looking at him! She was attractive and young, and John was getting extremely excited! Then she winked at him and smiled.

"Bill! Bill!" John whispered, "That girl is winking and smiling at me. What should I do?"

"Wink back at her and smile," Bill said.

So, John gathered up his courage and winked back at her and managed a slightly shy smile. Then nothing happened.

John looked back at her and to his surprise, the young girl was smiling at him and licking her lips!

"Bill! Bill!" John whispered. "She's smiling and licking her lips at me!"

Bill told John to smile back and lick his lips as well.

So, John gathered up his courage trying extremely hard to stay cool and smiled back and licked his lips. Then there was a pause and moments passed.

John glanced at her again. "Bill! Bill! She's leaning toward me showing me her tits! What the hell should I do?"

"Show her your nuts," Bill nonchalantly replied.

So, John turned toward her with both of his thumbs stuck in his ears, waving his fingers, and flapping his tongue said, "Flooogie, Flooogie, Flooogie!"

A neighbor hears a horrendous ruckus in the next apartment and calls the police. When the police arrive, they knock on the door of the apartment and a woman holding a bloody 5-iron lets them in. Directly behind her is a dead man lying in the middle of the floor.

The police are startled and check to see if the man is still alive. "He's dead," says one of the officers. "Ma'am, is this your husband?"

"That is correct, yes."

"Did you just hit him with that golf club?"

"Yes, I did." The woman breaks down and begins to sob uncontrollably letting the bloody golf club dramatically drop out of her hand and it hits the floor. She stands there with her palms covering her face continuing to cry.

"Wow, he's a mess! Can you tell me how many times you hit him?"

"I don't know... put me down for a five."

One for the 19th hole or delays on the course. Two Geriatricians were watching an old man hobbling down the sidewalk outside and noticed he was going awfully slow with his legs spread apart, and he was hardly bending his knees.

The first doctor said, "Looks like a serious orthopedic gait disorder. He's probably exhibiting early stages of Parkinsonism."

The other doctor didn't agree. "No, I suspect it's just arthritis. But he may be suffering from the adverse effects of medications due to polypharmacy including perhaps sedatives."

"I still believe it's probably Parkinsonism. He is walking too slow, and his legs are jiggling a bit and too far apart," said the first doctor.

"But it may be due to adverse effects from too many medications," said the other doc.

"Perhaps, but I'll bet you lunch on my analysis. Let's go politely ask him to see whose analysis is the closest to his condition."

They approached the old man and said, "Please excuse us, sir. We are geriatric doctors and do research and noticed your slow tedious and careful walk. We couldn't agree on the possible causes of your condition. Would you mind sharing with us what condition you have?"

The old man replied, “I’ll tell you what is wrong with me, but I would like to hear your thoughts first. Then, I’ll tell you if you are correct or not.”

The first doctor said, “I believe you may be suffering from the early stages of Parkinson’s disease. Or a problem with your central nervous system?”

“Sorry, but you have guessed wrong,” said the old man.

The second doctor said, “I believe it’s probably just arthritis you suffer from? Or perhaps adverse effects from medications?”

“Sorry, but you have guessed wrong also.”

“Well sir, please tell us what condition you have?”

The old man smiled, “I suspected I was going to fart…but I guessed wrong too.”

One for the golf club restaurant. After several weeks of trying, Joe finally got a beautiful co-worker to go out on a date with him. Joe spared no expense wanting to impress this beautiful woman and hired a limo, dressed up sharply, and brought her to the most expensive restaurant in town.

However, she was not impressed, and Joe realized she was out of his league and the conversation dwindled during awfully expensive dinner. Joe could tell she knew she was out of his league too. He excused himself and went to the restroom, but on his way there, he saw the beautiful actress, Cate Blanchett sitting with a group of friends. This gave Joe an idea.

"Ms. Blanchett, I'm very sorry to interrupt you but I thought you might help me in a matter of the heart?" The waiter came over, but Cate waved him off and said, "For a matter of the heart, I would love to. How can I help you?"

"See that beautiful woman at that table. See that woman at that table? I've been lovestruck with her ever since I first saw her. But this is our first date, and nothing is going right. Would you kindly stop by our table and pretend to know me and treat me like an old friend? She's a big fan of yours and it would catapult me to the top of her list, for sure!"

Cate laughed and said, "Sure, why not? Go and sit down and I'll catch her eye and notice you and head straight over to you." Joe couldn't thank her enough and made the trip back to his table. As soon as he sat down, he heard Cate shout, "Joe! Is that you?"

Joe's date looked up and said, "God! Is that Cate Blanchett!"

Joe nodded it was.

"Joe, why haven't I've seen you around the golf club?! Where on earth have you been?! I missed you so much! How long has it been?" Cate said as she approached their table.

Joe waved her off and said, "Listen Cate, I told you before – and I don't know how many times – but we're not getting back together! I wish you all the best and please, leave me alone. Thank you."

Dad pulled his son aside, "We need to have a talk son. In the years to come, you will have strong desires you haven't ever had before. Your heart will be pounding, your hands sweaty and you'll be totally consumed with passion."

"What are you saying, Dad? I think I know all that stuff."

"Please understand these feelings are perfectly normal. It's called golf."

Joe was in the bar having a drink with the rest of his foursome after a round when a striking woman walked in and sat down at the bar.

Joe was enamored and stared at her. She was wearing bright red, ultra-thin leather pants that were so tight it looked like they were painted on.

Joe got up and went over to her and stopped next to her admiring her pants wondering how in the world she ever got them on.

"Excuse me, Miss. I love your pants. But how on earth would anybody get into those pants?"

Grinning at him, she said, "Well, you can begin by buying me a drink."

Joe was 75 years old and extremely wealthy. His wife had died years ago, and he belonged to an expensive and very exclusive golf country club. One day, he walked into the clubhouse with a gorgeous and extremely sexy 22-year-old blonde. They turned everyone's heads as they strolled into the bar. She was draping herself all over Joe giving him her complete and undivided attention.

His friends at the club were astonished. They couldn't believe their eyes! When the blonde got up to visit the ladies' room, they asked Joe, "How the hell did you manage to get *her* as your girlfriend?"

"Oh, she's not my girlfriend, Joe replied, "She's my wife!"

They couldn't believe that and one asked, "Married? Wow! How did you do that?"

"Well, truth be told, I lied a bit about my age."

"What? Oh, I see, you're trying to tell us you told her you were only 50 and that beautiful creature believed you?"

Joe smiled and said, "Not at all! I told her I was 95!"

Van Gogh went into a bar and the barman asked him if he wanted a drink and Van Gogh said, “No, it's all right, I've got one ear.”

The late and well respected Seve Ballesteros was an excellent putter and player. When he was asked for the Spanish translation for what most golfers commonly refer to as a lag putt. Seve thought about it then asked what a lag putt was?

Seve had a great sense of humor, “I’d like to see the fairways made much narrower than they are at most golf courses, then everyone would have to play out of the rough, not just me.”

After Charlie retired, he played golf four times a week and neglected his wife. Being home alone a lot, the wife thought about getting a pet and decided she would like to find a talking and colorful parrot since it wouldn't be as much work as a dog or another pet and it would give her some company to hear it speak.

So, the wife went to a pet shop and looked around and a gorgeous multi-colored South American macaw caught her eye. She asked the owner if it talked and if it could talk.

"Oh yes, it talks."

"So how much for the bird?" She asked.

The owner told her $15.

"Why so cheap? What's wrong with it?"

"The bird is rude and vulgar. It used to be owned by a Madam who ran a brothel. It's not G-rated. More of a PG to R rated bird.

"Oh, I'll buy it anyway." The wife took it home in a large cage and kept it in the living room. The brilliant bird scanned the premises looking around. Then it finally spoke. "Oh, a new house with a new Madam."

The wife was taken aback some but didn't think that was too bad at all. At least he didn't use four-letter words yet.

The couples' three teen daughters came home from school and admired the bird in its beautiful cage. The bird looked at them and said, "Wow! A new house, with a new Madam, plus new whores."

The wife and her daughter were shocked at first, then had a brief nervous laugh about it.

Then Charlie arrived and the bird looked at him closely and said, "Wow!" A new house, a new Madam with new whores - just the same ol' same ol', Wait, hello again, how have you been, Charlie?"

Joe, a low handicap golfer, was going through his pre-shot routine before teeing off on the first hole. He stepped up to the ball and took a picture-perfect swing. Oddly, the ball began slicing terribly in the direction of the adjoining fairway. The ball struck another exceptionally large golfer who dropped to the ground completely unconscious.

Joe quickly drove up with his partner in their golf cart to the big man he just hit who was lying prone on the fairway with the ball just next to his neck and a large welt was developing on his forehead.

"Shit!" Joe exclaimed beginning to panic. "What the hell do we do now?!"

"Whatever you do, don't move him! He's too big to move but if we leave him here, I'll consider it an immovable obstruction under Rule 16. So, you can either play the ball as it lies or take a club-length drop no nearer the hole."

Joe visits his eye doctor to discuss his recurring headaches while reading. After examining his eyes, the eye doctor says, "Joe, you are generally fine, but it looks like you just need bifocals."

“Oh no!” Joe said. “I can’t play golf with bifocals! My handicap will go through the roof!”

"Well, you just need to use them when you read or play golf you can read, or you can play golf, but if you want to do both, you'll have to get bifocals."

The guy relents, gets his new glasses, then off to the course he goes. On the first tee he looks down and... behold...he sees a big ball and a little ball. He quickly decides to hit the big ball and puts it right down the middle. He does the same thing with his fairway shot, leaving the ball only ten feet from the cup.

Upon looking down before putting, he sees the big ball and the little ball. Then he looks ahead and sees a big cup AND a little cup. After a moment of strategic thinking, he decides to putt the little ball into the big cup and scores a birdie!

On the way to the next tee, he excuses himself to take care of business in the nearby trees. Upon his return, his partner notices that the front of his slacks is soaked from his crotch to his ankles.

"What the hell happened?" He asks.

"Well, I'm not sure," Joe says. "When I went over there to relieve myself, I pulled out a big one and a little one. Well, even though I wished it were, I knew the big one wasn't mine, so I replaced it back in my pants."

Joe was reading a magazine and noticed a golf resort ad where everything there is supposed to cost only $1. Playing golf, the drinks, the meals, rooms, etc. are all $1.

He decides to take them up on the offer and goes to the resort the next weekend.

Joe plays golf, has lunch and drinks, a massage, and enjoys all the facilities for only $1 each. On Sunday morning, he decides to play one more round of golf and at the pro shop, and he charges a sleeve of 3 golf balls to his room. Joe has a great final golf round on a beautiful day.

After the round, Joe checks out and goes over the bill and sees,

Golf: $1.00.

Drinks $1.00.

Dinner: $1.00.

Room: $1.00.

A sleeve of golf balls: $3,000.00

Joe can't believe his eyes and goes berserk and asks to see the manager immediately. The manager comes out of his office and greets Joe, "So sad to see you leave us, Joe. We hope you enjoyed yourself here?"

"Hey, don't give me the nice guy talk! You advertise everything here is only $1. Look at this bill! You are trying to charge me $3,000 for a sleeve of three golf balls?"

"Joe, I'm deeply sorry but there is no error here. If you carefully read our brochure and the rest of the information you were given when you checked in, you would have read what our golf balls cost."

Joe was even more upset now. “For this kind of money, I could have stayed at a much nicer resort that was totally upfront about everything. That’s crazy! $1,000 a golf ball! Why the place next door charges $1,000 a night for the ultra-luxury rooms and I could have stayed there at least knowing what I was paying for!"

"Yes, I completely understand your point and you could have done that. But the other resort across the street gets you by the luxury rooms while we over here get you by the balls!”

A young golf pro returned from his honeymoon with his new bride not talking to each other. The pro went to work the next day and his boss asked him, “How the honeymoon go?”

“Okay at first, but I was single for a long time and wasn’t getting used to being married yet.”

“What do you mean ‘Not used to it,’” said his boss.

“Well, after we finished having sex, I put a $100 bill on the pillow – it was just habit and I didn’t think twice about it.”

“Oh shit! Wow! You are in trouble. Maybe your wife will feel better with time?”

“Hell, I’m not concerned about her! The problem I have is, she left $95 change!”

A few stories about getting angry at yourself on the golf course.

We have all played with someone who has a temper. A few years ago, I played with a guy who was an angry man – just his nature. Incredibly angry, he would curse & yell over every missed shot or putt. On one hole he missed a 4-foot putt for birdie. He proceeded to punch himself in the face and knock himself out cold.

Another story. I broke a club only once. I was playing in a tournament, hitting the ball well, but three-putting every hole. I broke my putter over my knee and threw it in a lake, and as the shaft slid through my hand the jagged edge where I broke it cut the hell out of my hand. I finished the round with a towel full of blood putting with my 2 iron. I shot 81. I have calmed down ever since and never broke a club again. Lesson learned.

More stories,

- Played golf with a guy that bit himself so hard after a bad shot that he drew blood.
- Had a friend who turned up with a black eye. When asked what happened he

said, “I hit a bad shot, threw the club into the golf bag and it rebounded.”

- I played golf with a soldier with severe Post Traumatic Stress disorder. He was constantly cursing and throwing clubs all the time. On the fourth hole, his ball was behind a tree and he had absolutely no shot. He tried it anyway and of course, the ball hit the tree. He went crazy and attacked the tree with a golf club for about 20 seconds.

- My friend and I have a little saying for people we play with who constantly swear and throw their clubs. Usually calms them right down. I'll just say to them, “You're not good enough to get that mad.”

- I once played with a guy who got so mad, he broke his wedge in half. Then, he broke each half in half.

- I played with a guy who started literally pulling his own hair out in chunks on one of the greens.

- Although I wasn't a witness to this, I read years ago about a golfer getting so mad he threw his club as hard as he could at his golf cart. The club broke and part of the shaft rebounded and stabbed him in the chest

Dad brought home a robot having a lie detector feature that makes a siren sound and flashing lights when you lie. Dad asks his son, "Did you go to school today?"

"Yeah, sure!" The robot makes a siren sound.

"Okay, okay, I was reading and studying on my own." The robot makes another siren sound. "Okay, I went and played golf."

"When I was your age, I always went to school and didn't play hooky to play golf," Dad replies. The robot flashes lights.

"Haha!" Mom laughs. "After all he's your son." The robot makes a siren sound and flashes lights.

A golfer came home one evening to find his seven-year-old son polishing a new seven-speed bike.

"Son, where on earth did you find the money to buy such a beautiful bike? Wow! That is some bike! That must have cost $500 dollars!"

"Hi Dad! I earned it taking long walks."

"Long walks? What are you talking about?"

"Well, every weekend when you're out playing golf, our neighbor Mr. Brown comes over to see mom."

"What! Tell me more son."

"He gives me $25 and tells me to take a long walk."

A professor at a well-known medical school is lecturing to his class of medical students. The subject of the lecture is human anatomy and involuntary muscle response. He asks a woman student in the front row, "Did you know what your anus is doing while you are having orgasmic vaginal contractions?"

She replied, “First, I want you to clarify your question. Do you mean if I know what my asshole is doing when I’m having an orgasm?”

“Yes, that is exactly what I’m asking you.”

“He’s probably out golfing with his buddies."

Jim and Jane were happily married and they both enjoyed golf and they both enjoyed making love to each other and having sex very much. So, they made a secret pact between themselves. They promised each other that whoever died first would try to communicate to let the other know if there is sex after death and if they could play golf after death. They were very curious as both believed there wasn’t an afterlife.

After a long life together, Jim croaked and after a while contacted his wife, “Jane…Jane…”

"Jim? Is that you, Jim?"

"Yes, it's me and I've come back to tell you some things as we agreed."

"That's fantastic! What's it like?"

"I get up every morning, and I have sex. I have breakfast and then it is off to romp around the golf course and I have sex there too.

"Then I have greens for lunch and right after lunch, I go to the golf course again. I enjoy the entire course and I have sex for the rest of the afternoon as well."

"That's amazing Jim!"

"After dinner, I go back to the golf course and have more sex until night. Then I get a lot of sleep, and the lovemaking and golf begin the next morning as usual."

"Jim?"

“Yes, Jane.”

“Are you really in heaven?”

"No... I’m a rabbit in California!"

Bad behavior. John was a terrible 16-year-old who wouldn’t listen. He’d scream and yell on the golf course, throw clubs, and gave his father and mother fits all the time. He enjoyed driving them nuts.

One day the father came into John’s room and announced, “John, I have to tell you that you’ve been adopted.”

John exclaimed, “Adopted! Yes! I knew it! I must meet my biological parents!”

The father chuckled, "No, John, *we are* your biological parents. But start packing since the parents who have adopted you will be here soon."

One for the 19th hole. Bruce comes home late at night and stumbles around the house. He finally staggers into the bedroom. He's totally drunk. He wakes his wife, "Peggy, wake up! You won't believe this!

"What?" Peggy rises rubbing her eyes.

"I just came out of the toilet and...well, you really won't believe this, but the light automatically turned on all by itself!

After I was finished, again, the light automatically shut itself off! I didn't have to touch a switch! Am I getting psychokinesis superpowers or what!"

Peggy rolls over and moans, “You are absolutely disgusting. You just urinated in the refrigerator again!”

Joe comes home early from golf. His wife is surprised. “Why are you home? What happened?”

Pete and I aren’t playing golf together anymore.”

“But you’ve played together for years?”

“I know, I know, Joe said.

“Why?”

“Well, would you play with someone who cheats, has a foul mouth, throws clubs, makes a lot of noise just as you are about to make a shot, and doesn't pay the wager when he loses?"

"No way! That's terrible!"

"Well, neither will Pete!"

A foursome was playing the last hole in a $20,000 match and on the last green, one of the players had a 5-ft putt to win the hole and the match. He leaves it a half-inch short on the edge of the cup. Frustrated, he smacks the ball with this putter knocking it into the woods behind a large tree.

The other pair playing against him smile. One of them says, "Hey! We didn't give you that putt, so we win."

"Well, it's not over yet," the frustrated golfer says. "How about a side bet? I'll bet you double or nothing I can get that ball up and down."

His partner can't believe it. "Are you crazy? Your ball is behind a tree!"

"Okay, $40,000!" says the other pair quickly.

The frustrated golfer walks over behind the tree and says, "I declare this unplayable." He picks up the ball and replaces it on the edge of the cup and taps it in and says, "Now you owe me."

Rule 19. A player may take unplayable ball relief using one of the three options in each case adding one penalty stroke.

The player may take stroke-and-distance relief

Back on the line relief or lateral relief

Or play where the previous stroke was made.

Joe bought a new luxury SUV but brought it back to the dealer because he heard something like golf ball sounds coming from the trunk. The dealer gave him a new loaner and wrote the car up for repair,

"Customer reports a sound like golf balls are coming from the trunk."

Repairman writes up his report, "Cause is golf balls in trunk. Repair made; golf balls removed from the trunk."

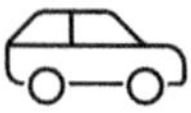

A woman is playing her very first game of golf with her husband who has just teed off and terribly upset.

The woman is about to tee off, but she hesitates and asks her husband, “So, what do I do? Do I aim for and hit it into the water?”

The husband is still fuming. “No! No! No! Don’t hit it in the water. Don’t even aim for the water. Aim for the short grass in the middle of the fairway.”

The wife is puzzled, “Why did you hit your ball into the water?”

“You don’t have to tell me I hit it in the water! I know that! I know! Look! Please listen to me. Please don’t hit it in the water since you try to avoid the water!”

The wife still puzzled, “So, why is there even water on this golf course if golfers shouldn’t hit the ball in the water?”

The husband loses it, “Because this is FUN!!”

I played golf recently with an old man who had a sweet swing on the range and must once have been an exceptionally good golfer. I respected his age, so we played from the whites.

On the first tee, he hit a nice draw about 190 yards to the middle of the fairway, then hit a 5-iron 150 yards to the middle of the green, and one-putted from 20 feet for birdie.

On the second hole, a par-3, he hit a hybrid 160 yards to the center of the green and one-putted from eight feet for another birdie.

“It's amazing how beautifully and easily you play,” I said. “You told me you're 95. That's hard to believe.”

“Thanks, he said. “I’ve been dreaming about this day for 10 years since the last time I played. My wife died and I didn’t do much for a couple of years because we always played together. She was a great golfer and could always see where the balls went, even when my eyesight started to go. Then I went virtually blind from cataracts and I couldn’t see anything. Finally, I decided to have cataract surgery a few months ago and get out on the course again. It’s so beautiful, with all the flowers and lakes and fresh air. I just love it.”

We drove up to the third hole and he hit another long drive, but this time the ball ricocheted off a tree on the right side of the fairway and bounced hard out of bounds.

“Fuck!” he screamed. “I hate this fucking game.”

John was away on a trip and after playing golf he was in the bar having a drink. His phone rings.

“Hello, Senor John? This is Juan the gardener.”

"Ah yes, Juan. What’s up?”

"I wanted to call you Senor to let you know your parrot has died.”

"Oh no! Not my special parrot? Died? The one that could talk in two languages?"

"Si, Senor, your special parrot died."

"Shit! That's terrible! I’m going to miss that bird. How did it die?"

"It ate rotten meat, Senor."

"Rotten meat? How did it ever eat rotten meat?"

"From a dead horse, and he ate the meat of it."

"Dead horse? Where did the dead horse come from?"

"Your racehorse, Senor. It died from pulling the water cart all morning."

"What the hell are you talking about? Why is my prize racehorse pulling a cart carrying water?"

"We needed the water to put out the big fire."

"What the fuck! What the hell happened over there? There was a fire?"

"A large fire happened at your house. The living room caught fire when a candle fell over."

"We have electric lights. Who was using a candle?"

“The candle was for the funeral, Senor.”

"What the hell are you talking about?! What funeral!"

"Your wife's, Senor...she died. She came home very late and since no one tries to get in the house that late, I thought she was trying to break in and I had to defend your home and I hit her with your new Driver."

Silence...

"Juan, if you even scratched that driver, you're fired!"

A husband and wife are sitting in the office of a marriage counselor after 20 years of marriage.

The wife is going on and on. "He golfs too much, drinks too much, eats too much, he's always gone, he's lazy, he neglects me, he doesn't listen to anything I say..."

Not saying a word, the counselor gets up and goes around the desk, and passionately takes the woman in his arms, kissing her repeatedly. The woman is stunned and totally silent.

The counselor turns to the husband and says, "What I just did is what your wife needs at least three times a week. Do you get the picture? Can you do that?"

"I can bring her in on every Wednesday and Friday, but on Monday, I play golf every week."

An old golfer was playing golf with his Minister and for the fun of it, they decided to play match play with the loser buying the other a beer. Even though the old golfer was much older than his young Minister, he was beating him bad and by the 14th hole, the old golfer won the match.

“I don’t know what it is,” Reverend. “I haven’t played this well in years.”

The Minister who was an accomplished golfer himself was not happy he lost the match so quickly to a much older golfer.

The old golfer saw how disappointed the Minister was and felt sorry for him and tried to cheer him up. “A young man like you are going to win many matches as the years go by. Just think, one day you’ll be giving the services at my funeral.”

The Minister tried to smile and said, “Yeah, that may happen, but it will still be your hole."

Two couples were playing their regular Sunday golf round. The men would tee off first then drive up to the ladies' tee box where the ladies would tee off.

After the men teed off on the 18th hole, the first lady on the ladies' tee took a wild and hard swing at the ball and whiffed it. She tried to hit it as far as the men just did and trumpeted a loud fart swinging with way too much force.

No one said a word.

Calmer now, she tried again, and this time lifted her head and topped the ball only to have it roll a few feet in front of her. When she did this, she let out another fart only a lot quieter this time.

Exasperated, she said, "I wonder why the ball didn't go very far"

One of the men said, "You needed more gas to give it a lot more gas!"

A couple recently got married and the new wife tells her new husband, "Honey, I've got a surprise for you! Shortly we are going to have 3 people here instead of just us two!"

"Wow! How wonderful! The new husband said then he embraced her very carefully and lovingly and kissed her several times with a big smile on this face.

The wife paused, "It makes me so happy you feel that way and tomorrow afternoon, my mother is coming to live with us!"

The husband didn't say a word.

When the husband came home the next evening after work, he kissed his wife and said, "Baby, I invited a friend over to join us for dinner this evening."

"What!" She exclaimed. "You're insane! This whole place is a mess, and I don't have enough food and most of the dishes are dirty and the other dishes are still in storage. Hell, I'm not doing any extravagant dinner!"

"I know. I know."

"Well, dear, why on earth would you invite someone over for dinner tonight?"

He replied, "Because the idiot is considering giving up the single life and getting married."

What does a golf cart running low on power and diarrhea have in common?

They make people think, "I'll make it back."

A devout Catholic confessed to a priest, “Yesterday I sinned with an 18-year-old girl.”

“For your penance, squeeze 50 lemons and drink the juice all at once.”

“Will that forgive all my sins, Father?

“No, it won’t. But it will completely wipe that dirty grin off your face.”

“Peter, what’s wrong? His friend asked as they sat in a bar over a beer.

“My wife is suffering from a heavy drinking problem.”

"I didn't know your wife was an alcoholic?"

"No, it isn't her. It's me, but she's the one who suffers."

One senior golfer said to another, "I'm starting to forget things."

"How long have you had this condition?"

"What condition?"

A man was getting his annual physical exam and his doctor asked him, "Do you engage in any dangerous sport?"

The man thought a bit, then said, “Well, sometimes I disagree with my wife.”

They both laughed. “Seriously, doctor, there are times when I feel like I’m being bossed around, well, almost bullied by my wife. Would you have any suggestions on how I can stop her from bossing me around?”

“You need to build up your self-esteem. Read this short paper on being assertive, and we’ll talk further about it at the next appointment,” the doctor said.

The man read the paper on the bus home and finished reading it just as he got off at his stop.

Storming through the front door of his house he walked right up to his wife and put his angry face an inch away from her face shouting, “Starting today, and I mean right now, I am the man of this house and whatever I say goes! And I don’t want to hear any complaints or gripes from you! None!”

The wife was startled.

He continued, “Starting right now, you are going to prepare an excellent dinner and when I’m finished, I will expect a beautiful dessert. When you are finished with that you are going into the garage and clean my golf shoes and my golf clubs since I’m golfing early in the morning. I’ll be home at 4 pm and expect you to have a warm bath ready for me. And, when I’m finished with my bath, guess who’s going to dress me and comb my hair?”

“I think the funeral director’s embalmers will be doing that,” replied the wife.

Sean Connery was an excellent actor and had agreed to do one more James Bond movie. The nefarious villain was supposed to be a doctor who is a proctologist.

The movie title was going to be, "Dr. Coldfinger" but it was canceled when the doctor pulled out.

Jim came home at 7 pm from work. When he opened the front door, the dining room table was elegantly set with two candles lit and a bottle of champagne in the ice bucket. His wife greeted him with a martini for him. She was wearing a seductive little black dress.

In a very sensual voice, she asked him. "Dear, have you ever seen a $50 bill all crumpled up?"

"No." Her husband said wondering but in good spirits joining in on it all.

She gave him a wink and a sexy smile then slowly reached with two fingers between her large breast cleavage and pulled out a crumpled $10 bill.

He took the $10 bill from her still wondering and smiling what was going on tonight.

"Have you ever seen a crumpled up $50 bill?

"No." He said now fully intrigued, smiling, and anxiously wondering where all this was going.

She gave him a wink and a very sexy smile and pulled up her dress showing her tiny, laced panties. She carefully reached into her panties with two fingers and came out with a crumpled $50 bill.

He began breathing heavily as he slowly took the crumpled $50 bill from her.

"Now," the very seductive wife said in a low sexy voice, "Have you ever seen $50,000 all crumpled up?"

"Wow! I like this," he said. "You got to be kidding!"

"Go look in the garage..."

One for the clubhouse bar. Dr. Vanessa Smith was a renowned sex therapist and a Medical Doctor who helped many couples with their sex lives. One thing about her that many people liked was that she would not take a case unless she truly felt she could help them.

The Jones came to see the doctor since their sex life was dull and boring. This was something that just happened over time.

She first went through giving them each complete physical and psychological examination and afterward, she told happily she would take them on for sexual therapy as she felt she could help truly them. The Jones were overly excited and looking forward to her much-needed help.

Doctor Smith told them that the first thing they were going to do was, "Go to the grocery store and buy a cluster of grapes and doughnuts. Then go home and strip off your clothes slowly in front of each other. Mr. Jones, I then want you to roll the grapes around your wife's vaginal area for 15 minutes and after that, leave one of the grapes in your wife's vagina. Then slowly retreat and crawl back to her like a lion and retrieve the grape in her vagina using only your tongue."

"Next, Mrs. Jones, I want you to take the doughnuts and separate 6 paces from your husband and play ring toss until you have a ringer on your husband's penis. Then, like a lioness, crawl up to him and slowly consume the doughnut."

The Joneses did as the Doctor instructed and within a few weeks, they were enjoying a wonderful sex life and even made up variations to it.

The Flugles were friends of the Joneses and learned about how Doctor Smith greatly helped them, so they made an appointment and went to see her.

Dr. Smith met with them and told them she would not take their case unless she felt she could help. They agreed so she gave them both complete physical and psychological examinations just as she did with the Joneses.

Then she told the Flugles the bad news. "I cannot help you. Please understand that I wish I could help you but as far as I can see, your sex life is as good as it will ever be. I am deeply sorry, but I cannot take you as patients."

The Flugles pleaded and pleaded with her and begged her for her help. "You greatly helped the Joneses, and they have an absolutely spectacular sex life. Please help us. Please?"

The good doctor thought about it for a while, then said, "Okay, go to the grocery store and buy several grapefruit and a box of Cheerios..."

There are made up jokes that are so dumb they're funny:

Bryson DeChambeau walks into a bar and gets a beer and notices there's a basket of roasted peanuts in the shell in front of him. He reaches for one, then hears a voice, "You are amazing, Bryson, you hit drives out of sight! You're the man! You're good looking too."

Bryson pulls his hand back and takes a sip of beer wondering about what just happened. He tries to get another peanut and hears, "Say you're really looking good, Bryson! You've been working out and the bulk-up looks great on you!"

Then he hears several voices, "That's Bryson DeChambeau! What a guy! He's smooth and smart! Women want him! What a catch he is!"

Bryson looks over at the bartender and says, "What the hell? There are voices coming out of the peanut basket?"

The bartender says, "Don't worry about it. The peanuts are complimentary."

Another one for the clubhouse bar. Sam was told by his doctor that unfortunately, he had only 24 hours to live. Understandably, Sam didn't go to work that day and came home and gave his wife, Penny, this tragic news.

Sam then asked Penny what most men would ask for when faced with their demise, he asked her to have sex with him.

Penny was deeply saddened by the incredibly sad news and being a good wife, she heartily agreed to have sex and they made love for the next 4 hours, then had lunch together.

After lunch, Sam asked Penny if they could have sex again, and Penny, although tired, agreed and they had sex until dinner time.

That evening after dinner, they had a sex session a third time and Penny was completely exhausted. They went to bed around 10 pm. Sam, although extremely tired, couldn't sleep and tossed and turned for several hours. In the middle of the night, he rubbed Penny's shoulder and said, "Penny, my dearest, I only have 4 more hours to live, could we have sex again? Just one more time? Please --"

Penny interrupted him, "Listen! I must get up in the morning. You don't!"

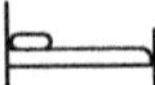

Joe was working awfully hard and spent a lot of time at work. He felt guilty about that and thought he would buy a small gift for his wife to show her he has been thinking about her and appreciates her.

He stopped at a large department store and went to the lady's department and thought a bottle of perfume might be the right gift. He asked the young clerk to show him perfume and she presented him with a genuinely nice bottle.

"This bottle of perfume is $50", she said to him.

"That's a bit much," Joe said, so she returned with a smaller bottle of perfume which had a price tag of $30.

"That's still quite a bit," Joe complained.

Getting a little frustrated, the cosmetics clerk brought out a tiny $15 bottle of perfume.

"What I mean is," said Joe, "I'd like to see something really, really cheap."

The cosmetics clerk handed him a mirror.

Frank sliced the ball off the first tee high in the air and the ball was headed directly at a group playing the adjoining fairway. The ball took one hop on the fairway then struck one of the players directly in the groin who then collapsed and was writhing on the ground in excruciating pain.

Frank got in his cart and quickly drove over to apologize. "I'm very sorry!" Frank said. "I hardly ever slice the ball and it took me by complete surprise and didn't have time to shout 'Fore!'"

"That's odd," the golfer groaned. "You had plenty of time to yell 'Fuck!'"

Joe was having a terrible day driving the ball. He sliced when he wanted to hit a draw, hooked it when he wanted to hit a fade, and topped the ball when he wanted to hit it straight. He asked the other guy he was playing with why he was playing so badly.

"Yes, I think I see the problem. There's a lump of crap on the end of your driver."

Joe pulled his driver out and cleaned the head of it.

"No," said the other guy. "The other end."

John was having trouble playing with his wife who talked and talked most of the golf round. On the last hole, he spoke up, “Jane, will you please shut up! You're driving me out of my mind!"

"That wouldn't be a drive," Joan replied. “That would be a ‘gimmie’ putt!”

Senior golfers were surveyed about difficulties in growing older. These were some of the questions.

Q. Where can men over the age of 70 find younger women who might be interested in them?

A: Try a bookstore, under FICTION, or have a few hundred dollar bills fall out of your back pocket.

Q: What can a man do during the very difficult times when his wife is having annoying hot flashes and experiencing menopause?

A: Keep busy. If you're handy with tools, you can finish the basement. When you're done and make sure you build it very comfortably as you will have a place to live.

Q: How do you deal with your wife having that terrible curse of the elderly wrinkles?

A: Take off your glasses.

Q: Seriously! What do you tell your wife to get rid of the crow's feet and all those wrinkles on her face?

A: Go braless. It will usually pull them out.

Q: Why do the 70-plus Champion Tour players use valet parking at golf tournaments?

A: Valets don't forget where they park your car.

Q: Is it common for 70-plus-year-olds to have problems with short term memory storage?

A: Storing memory is not a problem.

The current trend in humanity to do good in the world was improving and the devil was upset with a decline in the numbers of damned people condemned to hell. So, the devil decided to hold a meeting with demons. At the meeting, he asked his assistant demons for ideas to increase the numbers.

The devil called the meeting to order. "Should we give you all the refresher lessons on how to tempt better? All of you have been useless. You're not tempting humans strong enough. You waste your time down here roasting marshmallows, telling jokes, not achieving anything, or tempting people to sin. You are no good to anyone. What the hell are you going to do about it?"

One demon stood up and said, “Let’s tempt them to play a game to lift their spirits, make them feel they are on top of the world, and then suddenly dash them into deep depression unexpectedly and repeatedly. This will produce pain, frustration, and agony that would be so unbearable we will soon gain control of their wills!"

Another demon interrupted, "You mean golf?"

The devil said, "Wow! That’s good! But steady boys, we don't want to finish them off that quick."

Three guys were at the first tee waiting for Joe who they could see in the distance limping as he pushed his golf trundler to join them.

"Why are you limping Joe?" Asked one of them as he reached the first tee.

"It's an old football injury."

"I didn't know you played football, Joe?"

"Oh, I don't. I hurt my foot last year when I lost $1,000 on the Superbowl and put my foot through the TV."

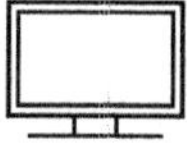

The internet is loaded fully on golf tips and golf advice. This was an actual question asked on Team Golfwell's Facebook group, Golf Jokes and Stories.

"I score anywhere between 47-52 for nine holes and manage to drink 6-7 beers on course. Any tips on how to improve my beer consumption?"

These were a few of the suggestions,

- "You may have an elbow problem doesn't bend enough. May need a professional to look at and give you some pointers."

- "Become the Beer Boy on the beverage cart."

- "Try to get paired up with the slowest members at the club. This will increase your time between shots thus increasing beer time."

- "Put a bottle of 100 proof schnapps or bourbon in your bag. Do a shot at every tee box and drink the beer on each hole while you look for your ball."

- "You can consume more if you get professional off-course training."

- "One swig per swing. Also, drench a clean towel in beer, then chew on it while walking."

The police broke up a prostitution ring at an exclusive Florida Golf resort on a late summer afternoon and lined up 10 girls they just arrested outside on the driveway entrance to the resort.

One of the girl's grandmother was going by slowly walking with her cane when she noticed her granddaughter standing in line. She stopped and ambled up to her.

"Why are you standing in line, my dear?" Grandma asked.

Not wanting to tell her grandma what was going on, she replied, "Grandma, the police are giving away free oranges and we are standing in line for them."

"Why that's awfully nice of them. I think I'll stand in line with you."

A policeman was going down the line asking each girl for identification and other details from all the prostitutes. When he got to Grandma he said, "Wow, grandma! You still going at this at your age? How the hell do you do it?"

Grandma smiled and said, "Oh, it's easy. I just take out my teeth and suck them dry." The policeman passed out.

Tony hit his ball into a ravine and went down the slope into the bushes to find it. The others lost sight of him.

After a moment, all they heard were "Crack, crack, crack..." and the sounds kept on and on. Finally, a golf ball came flying out of the ravine momentarily followed by Tony out of breath.

"How many times did you take getting the ball out?" One of them asked.

"Three," Tony replied.

"But I must have heard 8 or more?"

"Nine of them were echoes."

A young woman buys a dusty old mirror at an antique shop from a gypsy and hangs it on her bathroom door.

One evening, while she was getting undressed to take a bath, she jokingly chants,

"Mirror, mirror, on my door, make my bust line forty-four.

“And kindly add a Double D so I can’t see my golf ball teed".

Instantly, there was a flash brighter than a bolt of lightning and in the mirror, she sees her breasts enlarge to huge and incredibly beautiful breasts.

She’s happy as can be and runs with her huge new bouncing breasts to tell her husband what happened. The husband is overjoyed.

“Hey, that mirror might help me,” he said. She handed him the mirror and the husband took it into the bathroom and says,

“Magic mirror on this door,

“Give me a penis that will touch the floor.”

Again, there's a flash brighter than a bolt of lightning. He looks at the mirror and his legs are gone.

An engineer got hit by a bus and the next thing he knew he was standing before St. Peter in front of the pearly gates.

St. Peter was sitting at a desk going over things on his laptop. The engineer cleared his throat to get his attention. St. Peter looked up.

"Ah, you're the engineer. I see here you've been assigned to hell."

In an instant, the engineer is standing before a fiery cave and greeted by Satan himself.

Satan is holding a pitchfork with one hand and points the engineer to a large cave with flames shooting out of it. The engineer walks in.

After a while, the engineer gets bored with the place, so he designs and implements building improvements. He creates new land use designs to construct large developments. He puts in air conditioning in all structures, etc. Eventually, everyone in hell has a massive home with refrigerators, large swimming pools, and waterfalls. The engineer becomes extremely popular.

One day, God calls up Satan and asks, "How's it all burning down there in hell?"

"Hey, things are going great!" Satan says, "We've got air conditioning, new homes, swimming pools, hey, there's no telling what our engineer is going to come up with next!"

"What the hell? You've got an engineer? St. Peter must have fucked up again! Send that engineer back to heaven immediately." God said.

"No way! Everybody likes this guy, and I like the guy! And I'm keeping him!" Satan replied.

"Oh, yeah? How'd you like a thunderbolt up your arse!"

"I'd just jump in my pool, Haha!" Satan laughed.

"Listen you demon, you send him back up here or I'll sue you!" God said.

"Haha! Yeah right. You got lawyers up there... Haha...."

The groom to be is next to his bride to be at the church altar. The minister greets them and tells them to take a deep breath. As the bride exhales, she notices a set of golf clubs off to the side near the door.

“Those are your golf clubs, aren’t they?”

“Yes, they are.”

“What are they doing here?!” She asks.

“This isn’t going to take all day, is it?”

Bert finished his round and was at the clubhouse bar when a small Asian man came up next to him and started drinking a beer.

Bert asks him, “Do you know any martial arts like Karate, Taekwondo, Judo, Muay Thai, etc.?”

The small Asian man took offense. “What the hell? No, I don’t! Do you ask me these questions since I am Asian? You are a racist. I am Chinese and don’t know martial arts. Do you think all Asians know martial arts?”

“No, I’m not a racist. I just asked since you are drinking my beer!”

Golf Instructions for the Weekend Player.

1. Take a nice swing.

2. Curse.

3. Blame noise disturbance.

4. Blame golf course conditions.

5. Look for ball.

6. Drink beer.

7. Repeat.

Joe got finished with a very tough and long divorce proceeding and decided he would go out by himself and simply play a relaxing round of golf.

He watched a twosome in front of him throw an object in the bushes and walk off. When he passed the bush, he found it, rubbed it to get the dirt off and a genie popped out.

"Joe, I know you went through a tough time with your divorce. She dumped you after you worked hard, and she got most of the money. That's a common story. But you just can't neglect a woman. They deserve respect. So, to reward you, I'm going to give you the usual

3 wishes, but there was one special condition. Whatever you wish for, your ex-wife will get double of whatever you wish for."

Joe thought about it, then said okay and for his first wish, he wanted a Ferrari.

"Okay, Joe, but your ex will get 2 Ferraris."

"I don't care, as long as I get one for myself," Joe said.

Suddenly there was a flash and a brand new bright red Ferrari next to him in the fairway.

"My second wish is for one billion dollars," Joe said.

"Okay, Joe, but your wife gets 2 billion?"

"That's perfectly fine with me," Joe said.

Suddenly, Joe's phone vibrated showing his bank notified him he had 1 billion dollars deposited in his account!

"Only one more wish, Joe." The genie said.

"Sound good, genie. Here is my 5-iron. Please beat me half to death."

A minister asked a golf instructor after Sunday Services to play a round of golf with him.

"Sounds great, Reverend. I'll see you at the club!"

The minister was playing badly for the first 3 holes. The fourth hole was short par 3. "What are you going to use on this hole my son?" The minister asks.

The instructor replies, "A soft wedge, Reverend. What's your choice?"

"I'm going to use a 9-iron and pray." The minister said.

The instructor easily puts the ball on the green about 15 feet away. Then the minister tops the ball, and it dribbles off the tee only a few yards in front of him.

"What happened?" The minister asked.

The instructor replied, "I don't know about you Reverend, but when I pray, I keep my head down."

Bob, went on a camping trip deep in the forest with his wife, kids, and mother-in-law.

One evening, just before going to bed for the night, Bob's wife looks around and realizes her mother is gone! Rushing to her husband, she insists Bob try to find her mother right away!

Bob, his wife, and kids all search and look for her right away. One of the kids gets excited and motions all of them over. There, in a clearing not far from the camp, they all see a dramatic, chilling sight! Bob's poor mother-in-law is backed up against a tree and a large Kodiak bear is standing up on its hind legs facing her and growling ferociously.

The wife cries out, "Bob, do something!" Bob runs back and gets his 2-iron and takes a long swig of whiskey. He races back and studies the drama. The bear is now slowly circling the mother-in-law!

Bob steps back practicing his swing with the 2-iron several times, then pauses. "Shit, I'm not doing a damn thing! That poor bear got himself into this, so let him get himself out of it!"

A newly widowed woman calls the small-town newspaper office about an obituary for her recently deceased husband to arrange for an obituary. The newspaper office advises there is a cost of .75 cents a word.

Being frugal, she says, "Let it read, Joe Smith died."

The office tells her that's okay, but there is a seven-word minimum for all obits.

She thinks it over and, in a few seconds, says, "Have it read, 'Joe Smith died. Golf clubs for sale.'"

Golf Truisms:

- Golf is an extremely difficult sport to analyze. On some days, you duck hook shots, dribble drives, top the ball, slice shots into the water, take three shots to get out of bunkers, miss every green, and take 3-4 putts on every hole. Then for no reason at all, the next day you really suck.

- Football and Rugby are very rough sports where you must face exceptionally large and fearsome opponents. Golf is the only sport where the most feared opponent happens to be yourself.

- If you are trying hard to "shoot your age" you most likely will "shoot your weight."

- You consider all your good shots extremely skillful, but everyone else who hits good shots is only lucky!

- The higher your handicap is, the more you feel you could give great advice to the best in the game.

For the 19th hole.

After drinking a lot of beer in the bar at an exclusive golf club, a golfer developed a serious problem. He made several attempts to get into the men's room but found it locked so he used the ladies' room.

On his way out, he was greeted by an angry woman who shouted at him, “Excuse me, sir! This is for women!”

Unfazed, he pulled out his manhood and showed it to her and replied, “And so is this.”

Mrs. Smith complained to her doctor that her husband was golfing all the time. He competed on the club team, entered every tournament, totally neglected her, and literally gave her up for golf. They didn't have sex any longer as he was always too busy golfing.

"I have just the thing for you," the doctor said and gave her a bottle of white pills. "Put only one of these in his morning coffee and you should be 'satisfied.' No pun intended."

The next morning, she tried the pill out in his morning coffee, and in the evening, he kissed her romantically for 5 minutes.

The next morning, she put two white pills in his coffee, and that evening, they kissed for 10 minutes and caressed each other for another 10 minutes.

Still not "satisfied," she said, "What the hell" and put the entire bottle in his morning coffee. The coffee fizzed a tiny whirlpool form then dissipate.

A few days later, the doctor's office called to check on her progress.

A friend answered the phone. The doctor's nurse inquired how the woman was doing. A friend replied, "I just got here. She's unconscious lying on the floor with her legs sticking up in the air. All the women in the neighborhood are in the same state! He hasn't seen me yet, but he's running around naked on the front lawn yelling 'Where'd those chickens go?'"

Married golfers, according to a new study are generally heavier. Single golfers tend to be skinnier than married golfers provided they both play in the late afternoon.

After extensive study, it appears the single golfer has a "refreshment" after finishing a round, then comes home and opens the fridge and finds nothing there so he goes to bed.

The married golfer has a "refreshment" after finishing a round and goes home, then goes to bed and finds nothing decent there, so he goes to the fridge.

Joe went to the club manager complaining about women golfers driving golf carts.

"These two ladies barrelled past my cart full blast headed for the clubhouse and almost drove me into the lake on 18! They were both putting on their make-up! I yelled out but they just kept putting on their makeup or whatever!"

"Wow!" Who were they?" The manager asked.

"I didn't get a good look but they scared me so much I had to stop driving my cart and dropped my phone into the beer between my legs wrecking my phone, soaking my pants, and disconnected an important business call.

Joe won first prize at a golf tournament and received a free voucher for a visit to the local brothel. This is new to Joe as he hasn't been ever to a brothel but decided he would go in a week or so. He would have gone right away, but he was nervous about it having heard a lot of stories of extremely gorgeous women who worked there.

Sure enough, when he arrived, the girls paid a great deal of attention to him and he chose an incredibly attractive lady and retired with her to her room.

Shortly thereafter, she came running to the Madam and asked, "I haven't heard this word before so let me know what the client means when he wants a Mulligan?"

"More than anything else, golf itself puts pressure on the player. Competitors are not allowed to hinder you, as they are in other sports. The pressure originates in and by yourself. It builds up from doubts. A two-foot putt on the practice green doesn't spark many doubts. A two-foot putt to win a bet or a tournament or the Masters is another thing entirely."

-Joe Posnanski, The Secret of Golf: The Story of Tom Watson and Jack Nicklaus

A storm was moving while Joe was finishing his round. He was playing very well, and he thought this was going to be the best round of his life.

When he got to the 17th tee the wind had picked up making it difficult to even swing a club and as a result, he duck-hooked it into thick low bushes.

Miraculously he had a great lie, and although the ball was close to bushes, he could still make a swing. Dark clouds were moving in, so he set himself up quickly and just as he was at the top of the backswing, lightning struck down from the sky catching his steel-shafted 5-iron.

The rest of the foursome rushed over but Joe was gone and in his place was a dark deep crater. Joe was fried and dead as a brick.

When Joe reached the pearly gates, he was greeted by St. Peter who told him, “Joe, we are sorry to have taken you when you are still young, however, because you love to play golf, and you had the round of your life going, we decided to bring your clubs that you love so you can play all of the golf course here up in heaven. These courses are the epitome of golf courses and you will enjoy this incredible experience!"

Joe broke down and started sobbing uncontrollably.

St. Peter said, "Joe? I know, I know, you have left behind many loved ones."

"No, that's not it."

"Yes, my son, you also had led a good life, and enjoyed life very much I know you will miss it," St. Peter said.

"No, that's not it either," Joe cried.

"Well then, what on earth could make you so sad. Gosh, Josh, these are amazing and spectacular golf courses and you're crying like an extremely tired little boy?"

Joe looked up with tears flooding from his eyes, "I think I left my wedge back on the 16th green."

One for the 19th hole. A story about the different abilities each of us have.

On a small farm, a farmer lived with his wife and three sons. They were not financially well off; in fact, they were extremely poor and just had a single cow on their small farm.

One morning, the wife of the farmer woke up early in the morning and checked on the cow and saw it was stone cold dead lying in the field with its four legs sticking up in the air. She became depressed and despondent. How could they possibly continue to feed her family? She felt so hopeless and depressed, she hung herself.

When the farmer woke up, he saw his wife and the cow were both dead and felt very hopeless. So, in total despair, he put a gun to his head and shot himself.

The oldest son got up and saw both of his parents were dead and he saw the dead cow as well. He got depressed and yes, he also decided life was no longer worth living and went down to the river to drown himself but when he got there, he saw a mermaid sitting on the bank. He couldn't believe his eyes.

She said, "I'm a magical mermaid and I know the reason for your despair. If you will have sex with me several, let's say six times in a row, I will restore your parents and the cow to you." The oldest son agreed to try but couldn't have any more sex after four times so the mermaid let him drown himself in the river.

Next, the second oldest son woke up. He became depressed and despondent and started off to the river to end it all. The mermaid greeted him as well and said to him, "If you will have sex with me, let's say eleven times in a row, I will make everything right." And while the son tried his best (ten times!), the mermaid let him drown himself in the river.

The youngest son woke up and saw his mother and father dead. He became despondent and walked down to the river to throw himself in. He saw his two brothers also drowned. And then the mermaid greeted him.

"I am a magical mermaid and understand how you feel. I can make everything right and bring them all back to life if you will have sex with me, let's say twenty times in a row."

The young son replied, "Is that all? Why not twenty-five times in a row?"

The mermaid was taken aback by this request.

Then he said, "Hell, why not thirty-five times in a row?"

The mermaid didn't believe him and started to go away.

The youngest son said, "Why not FIFTY times in a row?!"

"Enough!" She said. "Okay, if you will have sex with me fifty times in a row, then I will bring everybody back to life, but I doubt you are going to do even half that."

"Wait," said the youngest son. "How do I know that fifty times in a row won't kill you like it did the cow?"

Another one for the Clubhouse bar.

Joe and John had just finished their golf round and on the way home, they stopped at the local County Fair. As they went through the entrance, they saw a crowd gathered and they went up to them.

"What's going on?" Joe asked one of the bystanders.

"Some crazy guy is trying to ride the super bronco machine." Joe noticed this huge foreboding machine. "Nobody has been able to stay on for the full three minutes. They had to take one guy away on a stretcher."

“That’s not for me. Let’s go have a beer.” John said to Joe.

The bystander continued, “If anyone can stay on it for 3 minutes, they win $1,000.”

“I’ll try!” Joe said.

“Joe, are you crazy? Look at that thing! You haven’t ever ridden a horse in your life!” John said.

While they were discussing it, another guy jumped on it trying to ride it but shortly after the machine was started, he was hurled ten feet in the air and had to be taken away in an ambulance.

“I can do this!” Joe said. “Watch this!” Joe climbed aboard the machine.

The machine jerked wildly up and down, sideways, in loops and circles, but Joe was still hanging on. Then after a minute, the machine was jerking straight up and down, spinning super-fast and Joe just became a blur.

When 3 minutes were up, Joe was still miraculously sitting on the machine! The crowd had grown to an exceptionally large size and all were wildly cheering and applauding! Joe collected the $1,000 prize and gave the crowd a friendly wave.

John was stunned. He went over to him. “Joe, you okay? That was amazing! How did you learn to do that?”

“Remember when my wife and I first got married? I used to come up on my wife from behind, mount her, and reach around and place both of my hands on her breasts, and say, “Your sister has bigger ones! Then I kept trying to stay on for 10 seconds!”

Charlie was playing a long par 5 and hit a big drive off the tee that sliced into a large stand of trees. He searched for his ball and found it in the stand of trees. He had a good lie but there wasn't much room to hit between the trees. He decided to give it a try.

He studied the shot carefully then took out his three-metal and made a smooth swing only to have the ball strike the tree in front of him and ricochet backward striking him right between the eyes killing himself instantly.

The next thing he knew, he was in front of St. Peter before the pearly gates. St. Peter asked him, "Charlie, are you a good golfer?"

Charlie thought about it then said, "Got here in two, didn't I?"

Angus and Callum were sitting in the clubhouse after finishing golf on a cold nearly freezing day. It was raining heavily, the winds gusted to gale-force speed. Lightning strikes were everywhere!

They both had ice in their hair, ears, and their long beards. Freezing rain beat rhythmically on the roof and windows. They didn't say anything as they gazed into their scotch sitting by the fireplace until Angus said, "That was a very good round of golf."

"Aye, I think we both played very well," Callum said. "Same time next week?"

"Aye," said Angus, "Weather permitting."

An Australian golfer was talking to his barber while getting a new haircut for his upcoming trip to the Masters Golf Tournament in Augusta. He was overly excited about the trip and taking his wife to the US.

The barber asked, “Why the hell would you want to go to the US? It’s tough getting through Customs and you’re going to be standing in lines for hours in dirty crowded airports surrounded by cranky tired people after a long boring flight?”

“We’re going through Los Angeles on Qantas.”

“Well, in my opinion, LAX is the worst, and Qantas? Mate? They’re also bad news in my opinion. The flights are not on time, the food stinks, and the flight attendants couldn’t care less. They are awfully slow!”

The barber continued speaking as he was cutting hair. “It’s better to watch the Masters Golf Tournament on TV, mate. It’s too crowded over there. You’ll be standing way back and several rows deep and won’t see much. There are long queues for everything especially the portaloos. Save your money, mate! TV is a lot easier. By the way, there hardly any hotels over there. Where are you staying?"

"The tour guide has that all arranged."

"Yeah, tour guide, sure. He'll give you each a pillow and put you both in a toilet and charge you for the Taj Mahal. He just wants your money. And they don't care about repeat business."

Three weeks later, the customer returned after the trip for another haircut. The barber asked him how it went.

"It was wonderful, the golf was fantastic! Not only were we on schedule in one of Qantas' brand-new planes, but it was overbooked, and they bumped us up to first class. The food and wine were wonderful, and I had a beautiful flight attendant wait on my wife and me hand and foot. She even brought us a nightcap."

“Okay. How were the airports?”

“We got through LAX easily – no problem. And the hotel was great! They'd just finished a multi-million-dollar super renovation, and it’s the finest place in the area. The hotel was overbooked, so they gave us the Presidential Suite at no extra charge! We even had a butler who accompanied us to the golf tournament and waited on us, all compliments of the hotel!"

"Well," muttered the barber, "You just got incredibly lucky. But I know you didn’t see any of the player interviews?”

“We followed Adam Scott and his caddy, a Kiwi, you know, Steve Williams. The tour guide made sure we were always upfront, and we could see it all! We even saw Adam’s putt go in on the 10th green to win the playoff!”

“When Adam walked off the green after the celebration, the Adam noticed us and told something to Steve, and Steve came over and told us Adam was so grateful all the support, and he could tell we were Aussies when he heard us cheer. Steve said Adam really appreciated our support coming from so far away and invited us to go with him into the clubhouse to see him receive his first green jacket."

"Are you shitting me?" The barber said.

"So, we went into the clubhouse with Adam and witnessed him getting his green jacket. Then Adam came up to my wife and I and talked with us."

"Wow! Really? What did he say to you?"

He said, "Who fucked up your hair?"

Here are things your gorgeous lady golf partner wouldn't ever say to you,

"Do you really want to finish? I'd like to go someplace quiet and get intimate right now. I'm tired of just being friends."

"I think all of the thick hair on your butt is very sexy."

"Wow! Turn on the fans and abandon golf cart! Did you get a whiff of that one I just blasted!"

"Please don't throw that old golf shirt away, the holes showing your thick chest and armpit hair are just too cute."

"I like it when you don't use deodorant. That turns me on!"

"This diamond is way too big."

"Wow, it really is 11 inches!"

"Do these plaid shorts make my ass look too small?"

"I'm totally wrong, you must be right again."

Joe, John, Peter, and Frank were approaching the tee on a 464-yard par-4 of a golf course they hadn't ever played before. As they stood on the tee, they saw the dead straight fairway was next to a road that ran down the right side of the entire length of the hole. The green was slightly to the left of the straightaway hole.

The first three teed off then Joe hit fourth and sliced a long drive toward the road. Joe's ball went over the fence, bounced 50 yards down the road, where it stuck in the tire rim held by the centrifugal force of the bus wheel and later rolled out as the bus slowed and bounced and rolled back on the course stopping just 10 yards short of the green.

As they all stood in amazement, John asked, "How on earth did you do that?"

Joe said, "You have to know the bus schedule."

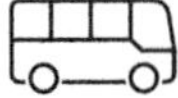

Years ago, Peter and Frank decided to attend a golf tournament to see the best golfers competing. They enjoyed themselves watching the pros and liked drinking beer. After a few beers, Peter had to find the public men's room and it had a long line of urinals. Peter went in and there is only one other man who came in and stood next to him. Peter noticed the man had no arms.

As Peter was doing his own business, he wondered how this unfortunate man was going to urinate. He finished and was washing his hands when the man asked Peter to help him.

Peter felt sorry for the guy and said, "No problem, I see what I can do."

The guy says, "Are you able to unzip me?"

Peter says, "Sure," and unzips the guy's trousers.

Then the guy says, "Please sir, will you pull it out for me?"

Peter says, "Okay." Then it gets very strange. He pulls the man's willy out. His will is bright red with dark gray patches and covered with red bumps, puss filled pimples, scabs, and smells terrible.

Then the guy asks Peter to aim it toward the urinal catch basin and Peter points it for him.

The man finishes urinating. Peter puts his willy back in the guy's pants and zips him up.

"Thank you very much. That is genuinely nice of you and I really appreciate your kindness."

Peter says, "No problem, but there is something seriously wrong with your willy."

The guy pulls his arms out of his shirt and says, "Yeah, I agree, and I don't know what's wrong, but I ain't touching it."

A beautiful LPGA golfer is seated next to a professor on a long flight.

The professor makes small talk with her, then asks if she would like to play a fun game?

The lady pro was very tired, and just wanted to sleep and she declined, then she closed her eyes trying to get a nap.

He didn't give up and explained that the game is a lot of fun.

He said, "I ask you a question, and if you don't know the answer, you pay me $1.00, and vice versa."

"No thank you," she murmured.

The professor, now irritated, says, "Okay, if you don't know the answer you pay me $1.00, and if I don't know the answer, I will pay you $100.00."

The lady pro opened her eyes. Thinking she can't stop the persistent professor, she reluctantly agreed to the game.

"I'll ask the first question," The professor says. "What's the distance from New York to LA?"

The lady pro doesn't say a word, reaches into her purse, pulls out a $1.00 bill and hands it to the professor. She closes her eyes and tries to sleep.

"Okay" said the professor, "Your turn."

She opened her eyes and asked, "What golf course has 17 holes but is still a regulation golf course?"

The professor is puzzled. He taps into the phone on the plane with his modem and searches the net and other sources, no answer.

He sends emails to all his colleagues and students, but no one knows.

After an hour and a half, he wakes the pro, and hands her $100.00.

The pro says, "Thank you," and turns away to go back to sleep.

The professor is pissed. He wakes her up and says, “Well, what's the answer?"

The pro reaches into her purse, and hands him $1.00, and goes back to sleep.

Fred played a lot of golf and usually played with his wife. But one day at the club, he was playing alone with his dog along.

Joe saw Fred on the tenth tee and stopped him. “Fred, what the hell is going on? For years I’ve seen you play with your wife and now you’re with your dog? Is your wife okay?”

“Yes, she’s fine. She said she doesn’t want to play golf with me anymore. So, I bring my dog.”

“Your dog? Why do you play golf with your dog?”

Fred thought about it then said, “First, if you’re late, the dog is always excited to see you. And it’s okay if you call the dog by another name.”

“I get the picture,” Joe says.

"Not the whole picture, "Dogs don't care if you're a slob. You'll never be visited by the dog's parents either. Dogs like the outdoors. If a dog has a litter you can put an ad in the paper giving them away. Dog's don't care if they smell another dog on you, they just find it curious."

"You are sounding very strange, Fred," Joe says.

"Oh yeah? Doesn't it make sense to you to know if a dog leaves, it won't take half the stuff you worked for? And, more than anything, if you mistakenly lock your dog out of the house, he's still overjoyed to see you."

Joe came home from golf and heard his three small children shouting in the back yard and rushed through his side gate and found his children in the back yard in their pajamas, sitting in the mud, throwing mud at each other and just out of control.

After he calmed them all down, he hosed them down then brought them inside. The back door was wide open. The dog was nowhere to be found.

He went into the kitchen and the sink was filled with dishes, dog food was all over the floor, milk and orange juice were spilled all over the counter and the refrigerator and freezer doors were wide open. He kicked his way through empty cereal boxes, bowls, spoons, and a ton of mess. He called out for his wife, but there wasn't any answer.

Walking into the hallway, he kicked his way through a larger mess. The tall pole lamp from the living room had been kicked over, pillows from upstairs were strewn all over the floor. The television was on with cartoons blaring away. Toys were everywhere. It looked like a tornado had gone through the home!

He rushed up the stairs, fighting his way through piles of clothes and more toys, very worried something happened to his wife.

At the top of the stairs, he saw water dripping out of the bathroom sink making puddles on the floor. There were wet towels, scummy soap, and more toys strewn over the floor. A trail of toilet paper led to a heap and toothpaste had been smeared over the mirror and walls.

He rushed into their bedroom and found his wife still curled up in the bed in her pajamas with headphones on listening to music and reading. She smiled when he came in and took off her headphones and asked about his day.

He looked at her, totally bewildered, and asked, "What happened?"

She smiled, "You know dear, every day when you come home from work and you ask me what 'in the hell' I do all day?"

"Yes?"

"Well, today I didn't do it!"

"I have experienced what laughing can do."

"It transforms almost unbearable tears into something bearable, and almost hopeful."

-Bob Hope

Joe's wife couldn't sleep. She was wide awake at 3 am sitting downstairs in the lounge with a small lamp on writing in her diary,

"My husband is not himself and acting very strange. We met for dinner tonight at our favorite restaurant and traffic was heavy and I was late and thought I would hear a slide remark, but he didn't mention it at all.

"We were having a dangling conversation over dinner and he kept to himself all evening. I asked him what was wrong.

"He said, 'Nothing.'

"I thought there was something I did wrong, so I asked him if I made him upset. He said he wasn't upset and not to worry about it.

"As he was driving home, I told him, 'I love you.'

"He smiled and nodded and just kept driving. This wasn't the Joe I know. He always says, 'I love you too.'

'When we got back, he acted like he didn't want anything to do with me. He sat and watched TV completely detached, distant, and didn't want anything to do with me.

"So, I went upstairs and went to bed. Thirty minutes later he came to bed but didn't touch me. His head was somewhere else.

'He fell asleep and I cried. What can I do? I'm sure we are growing apart. My life is ruined. What did I do?"

The husband's diary said, *"A one-foot putt. Who the hell misses a one-foot putt?"*

For the 19th hole. "Wow looking good!" Mike said as he saw John walk into the office one morning. "That's a great looking suit. You must have an important meeting today. Where did you get it?

John smiled. "No, the Mrs. got it for me. It's pretty nice made up of exceptionally fine wool – the kind, you know, you get from stores I don't ever shop in."

"Do you know where she got it?"

John chuckled, “I don’t know and I’m not one to look a gift horse in the mouth.” He shrugged, “I just came home from work early the other day and there it was, hanging over the chair in the bedroom.”

A lawyer sends his good clients who enjoy golf a dozen Pro Vs with his name printed on each ball every Holiday Season.

A client thanked him in an email and added a P.S. “This is one of the rare occasions when I’ve had a lawyer *buy* the balls.”

Another one for the 19th hole. Fred and Paul took a golfing trip to Orlando, Florida, and loaded up Fred's SUV with their golfing equipment and headed south.

Unfortunately, they'd been so busy planning the trip they didn't see or hear all the warnings of a large storm coming in off the Atlantic Ocean heading straight for the Orlando area. The weather got terrible with heavy rains and strong winds.

They had no choice but to get off the road and pulled into a nearby country ranch at night as the weather was getting worse. An attractive mature lady answered the door and they asked if they could spend the night.

"I understand the weather is terrible and the ranch house has ample room for you," she said. "But my husband just passed away and I don't want my neighbors telling stories about me if you stay in my home."

"No worries, we'd be happy to sleep in the stables and we'll be gone early in the morning as soon as it's light," Fred said.

The nice lady agreed, and they set themselves up in the stable and settled in for the night.

By morning, the weather cleared, and they enjoyed a great weekend of golf.

Several months later, Fred got a letter from a lawyer. He couldn't figure it out at first then realized this was a letter from the lawyer for the estate of the attractive mature lady who allowed them to sleep in the barn on that stormy night before their golf weekend.

Fred called Paul and asked, "Remember that attractive lady on the ranch who let us stay in her barn on that stormy night on our trip to Orlando?"

"Yes, I remember her," Paul said.

"Paul, after I fell asleep in the stable, did you get up and go to her house and, well let's say, 'tuck her in' that night?" Fred asked.

"Yes, I did! I went over to her house and she was incredibly happy to see me. She was all over me! A fantastic evening."

"Okay, I think I get it now," Fred said. "Paul, did you happen to tell her my name instead of yours?"

An embarrassing pause followed. "Yes, Fred I told her I was you and gave her your name. Why are you asking about this now?"

"Nothing," Fred said. "She just passed away and left me everything."

Frank got a bit depressed hearing all the sex stories from the other three in his usual

Saturday foursome. Seems he was the only one having severe problems with his sex life, so he thought he would seek professional help and made an appointment to see a psychiatrist.

The psychiatrist asked him many questions and it took three full sessions for the psychiatrist to truly learn about Frank and his somewhat normal background. However, the good doctor just couldn't determine exactly what was causing Frank to have so much trouble with having sex.

Out of desperation, the psychiatrist asked Frank, "Do you ever watch your wife's face while you're having sex?"

"Well, yes, I did once," Frank replied.

"Tell me how she looked to you."

"Extremely angry," Frank said.

The psychiatrist finally felt he might be getting somewhere and asked, "That's intriguing. Let's delve further into this. You say you only saw your wife's face one time while having sex?"

"Yes, that's correct."

The doctor paused and looked through a reference book he had on his desk. He read something, then shut the book. "Frank, that is very unusual to only see your wife's face one time during sex. Tell me how it occurred where you saw your wife's face one time while having sex."

"Well, she was looking through the window at us."

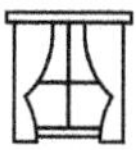

Ever hit a tree? There is now a new very friendly rule about trees for recreational golfers only.

Any ball that hits a tree is deemed not to have hit the tree since a ball striking a tee is bad luck and trees have no business being on a golf course after the player has paid money to play the golf course. If a player's ball strikes a tree, the player should in good faith estimate the spot to where the ball should have reasonably traveled to had it not hit the tree and place the ball on that spot and play the ball from there without penalty.

Ever lose a ball? A new friendly rule for recreational golfers only.

Lost balls are no longer counted since the ball will eventually be found someday by someone. Whoever finds the ball will usually keep the ball. Any player who loses a ball does not incur any penalty as the player is already out of pocket for the expense of the ball that he owned. The player should place a ball to the place he reasonably estimates where the ball should have gone and then play from there. This new rule is designed to speed the pace of the game and make it more enjoyable. Well, anyway it doesn't hurt to dream up these new rules.

"It is not true that people stop pursuing dreams because they grow old, they grow old because they stop pursuing dreams."

- Gabriel García Márquez

Jane went to the course hoping to play with another woman. She hung out in the pro shop when another single woman walked in to inquire about golf.

The pro introduced them and gave them a tee time in a few minutes. While waiting, the first woman asked the second, "What's your handicap?"

"Oh, I'm scratch," the other replied.

"Wow! I haven't played with someone who plays even with the card very much. That's very impressive! How long have you been a scratch golfer?"

"Ever since I started playing. I write down the good scores and scratch out the bad ones!"

There's an old story about an old PGA Tour golfer. He hired a new caddie before the British Open since he wanted someone with local knowledge, but he hated any distractions.

He told the new caddie, "Look I want you to keep your mouth shut and no matter what happens, don't say anything unless I ask."

The caddie politely answered, "Yes, Sir, I completely understand."

On a long and narrow par 4, the golfer pushed his tee shot right into deep rough and was 180 yds out to a two-tiered green with the pin in the back-right corner. The golfer took an iron and with a mighty swing hit a high fade to about a foot from the pin. He looked at the caddie and with much excitement and said, "Did you see that shot, that was a magnificent shot right?"

The caddie didn't say anything.

"Look I give you permission to say something, wasn't that a fantastic shot!"

The caddie answered, "Yes, sir, it surely was but you hit the wrong ball. If you look here, this is where your ball is."

Another one for the 19th hole. Joe's wife says to him, "Sweetheart, I have to confess when I'm having sex with you, I think about other men."

Joe replies, “Oh, you don’t think of me?”

“Yes, Joe, I just want to be completely honest with you. Deeply sorry.”

“Well, when I have sex with other women, I’m thinking about you!”

Joe walks very strange now but should be back to his old self once his injuries heal.

A few short ones for delays on the course.

What's the difference between a golfer and a skydiver?

A golfer goes “whack” then "damn," and a skydiver goes "damn" then “whack.”

*

A set of golf clubs walks into a bar. The bartender asks the biggest one, “What’ll you have?”

The golf club replies, “Nothing, I’m the driver.”

*

Four ladies were about to tee off. Suddenly, out of nowhere a naked man sprinted across the fairway in plain sight right in front of them.

They all gasped. One of them said, "Hey, I think I know that guy – it looked like, well, I’m not sure, but isn't that Dick Green?"

"No," replied another lady, "I think it's a reflection of the grass!"

*

Mike was having a terrible day and he and Bob just finished the front nine.

Bob asked him, “You're not your old self today, what's the matter, Mike?”

Mike, looking glum, said, "I think my wife’s dead."

"Wow! That's terrible! said Bob. “Wait a minute, you say you *‘think’* your wife is dead! Why aren’t you’re sure whether your wife is alive or not?”

"Well the sex is the same, but the dishes are piling up."

*

The manager at an exclusive golf club asks his assistant manager. “Say, have we had any response yet to our ad for a night guard?”

“Yeah, the pro shop was robbed last night.”

*

A guy and his wife are waiting for a long-anticipated boxing match to start on TV. The husband has a cooler by him with plenty of beer to enjoy during the match.

His wife says, “You really going to drink all that beer?”

The husband doesn’t respond as the bout finally begins.

Shortly the husband says, “What the hell! That was disappointing! It only lasted 40 seconds!”

He knocked him out in 20 seconds!”

“Yep,” replies the wife. “Now you know how I always feel.”

*

A husband and wife are sitting at home in the evening watching television.

The husband is drinking a glass of his favorite beer and the wife is drinking a glass of her favorite wine.

Suddenly, the husband says, "I love you."

Surprised, the wife says, "Is that you or the beer talking?"

"This is me talking to the beer."

A professor at a well-known medical school was lecturing his students on how to perform a self-exam on the breasts and testicles.

After class, one of the lady students asks Paul, another medical student, "Do you get an erection when you examine your testicle?"

"Not always, but some of the time," he replied.

"If you do get an erection, what do you do?"

"I don't do anything," he said.

"You mean to tell me you go around with an erection all day long?"

The young male student was taken aback. "Why, no."

She was getting a little upset. "Are you telling me if you get an erection, it will go down all on its own?" She asked.

"Well, yes," he said.

She was furious and said, "I'm going to kill my husband!"

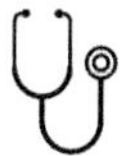

Missing short putts can lead to brain damage if you take golf too seriously. A masochist and a sadist teamed up for a Two-Man foursomes' tournament, and they almost won the whole tournament, but the masochist missed a one-foot putt to win on the 18th green.

The masochist pleaded and pleaded with his sadist partner, "Please hurt me... hurt me for missing that short putt!"

"No," replied the sadist.

Joe was having a terrible day on the course. He was playing foursomes in teams of two and caused a loss on almost every hole. After he missed a one-foot putt to lose another hole, his partner asked him,

"This isn't like you, Joe. You make those one-footers in your sleep. What's going on with you?"

"Shit! It's the wife" said Joe. "As you know, she's taken up golf, and says she loves the game – she's always gone. And, ever since she's been playing, she's cut my sex down to once a week."

A guy on the other team overheard and said, "You should consider yourself really lucky, Joe,"

"What do you mean?" Joe asked.

"Hell, she's cut some of us out altogether!"

Gary is at the golf clubhouse bar looking at the ladies in the room and thinking about sex. He loved his wife but had difficulties not wanting relationships with other women. He began mumbling to himself, *"Not worth it. It's never as good as the imagination. Expensive and above all drives the wife berserk."*

A friend of his was sitting nearby and overheard him. He came over and put his arm around him and said, "Come on Gary you knew what to expect when you took up golf."

Bill teed off on the first tee and sliced it terribly over a home's roof. He wasn't going to look for it since it was way out of bounds and there was not much chance of finding it anyway.

After finishing nine holes, the pro runs up to him. "Bill, wait a second, please."

"What's going on?"

"When you teed off on the first tee your ball bounced on the roof of the house and into the road and crashed through the windshield of a car. The guy was taken to the hospital and we hear he is in serious condition."

"Woah! I didn't mean to do anything like that. You guys ought to have a protective screen to stop balls that are sliced."

"For you to hit the house, you not only sliced but were totally misaligned."

Just then, the pro's phone rang. He answered the call and listened. He hung up and said, "Bill, I've got some awfully bad news. The driver of the car has just died. I think you better notify your insurance."

"Insurance? I don't have insurance for that! No way. What the hell?"

Bill was sued for several million dollars and as the Judge approved the jury's verdict against him for $10,000,000, the judge asked Bill what he was going to do about it."

"Well, your honor, the next time I'm going to roll my right hand over so I can see at least two knuckles on my right hand."

"The greatest thing about golf is there's no end to it unless you're dead."

"You just go from here to the Senior Tour."

- Fuzzy Zoeller

Just out! A scientific new study had some interesting conclusions on the and BMI and weight of golfers in a particular summer industrial golf league. The research indicated that unmarried golfers who play in these leagues are 'skinnier' than married ones.

The study's explanation for this surprising result was intriguing and a first in science!

The unmarried golfer plays his round of golf, has a “refreshment” at the 19th hole, goes home and goes to his refrigerator, finds nothing decent there, and then goes to bed.

The married golfer plays his round of golf, has many beverages at the 19th hole, goes home and goes to bed, finds nothing decent there, so he explores the refrigerator.

It was terrible outside. Lightning, thunder, yet Sam and a friend were determined to play. Sam was struck by lightning on the third hole, died, and went to heaven.

St. Peter greeted Sam and told him a mistake was made since the bolt of lightning was really meant for his golf partner. He said he talked to God about it and God said to cover it up as God does not people to know that mistakes from heaven happen from time to time. So, St. Peter told Sam he could go back to earth, but he had to be someone else other than himself to make sure this wouldn't get out.

Sam thought about it for a while and told St. Peter that he wanted to return to earth as a lesbian.

St. Peter was surprised. "What the hell? A lesbian? That's a new one! Why would a macho guy like you want to be a woman and a lesbian?"

"It's really simple Pete, and I'm surprised you don't get it. This way I can still make love to a woman, AND I can hit from the red tees!"

Fred went to Africa on business and arranged his schedule to arrive early so he could enjoy a round of golf in Africa. The course he wanted to play was in the middle of the jungle and when he checked in at the pro shop, he told the Pro he wanted to play 18 holes.

"Yes, no problem," said the Pro, "There are no other players right now, so hope you don't mind playing alone?

"No, that's fine," Fred said.

"Okay, we'll get you a caddy. Oh, what's your Handicap?"

"It's 16," Fred said, "But since I'll be playing alone, why does that matter?"

"No, trust me, it's important for us to know," said the Pro.

The Pro called a caddy in from outside and told him to show Fred the course. He also told the caddy as they left, "His handicap is 16."

Fred didn't know why his handicap was such a big deal. So, he just ignored it.

The caddy had a high-powered hunting rifle strapped over his shoulder and picked up Fred's bag and led the way to the first tee.

On the first tee which was a long par 4, the caddy said, "Keep it away from the trees on the left side and you'll be fine."

Fred hooked his drive into the trees that he was told to avoid and went in the trees found his ball. Just as he chipped out, he heard the loud crack of a rifle, and a huge snake fell from a tree branch just above him.

Fred looked at the snake and said, "Holy Shit!"

"That snake is poisonous and would have nearly killed you. I think you know now why I carry the rifle," said the caddy.

"Thank you," Fred said.

Fred double-bogeyed the first hole. The second hole was a par 5. The caddy told him, "Keep it away from the bushes on the right."

The caddy's remarked bothered Fred, who hardly ever slices, and, of course, he sliced it into those bushes. He found his ball and was about to take an unplayable lie when he heard the loud crack of the caddy's rifle and a lion fell dead right in front of him.

"Holy fucking lion shit!" Fred exclaimed.

"Glad I got him. He would have eaten you."

"Thanks man!" Fred said.

On the short par 3 third hole, Fred ball came up just short of the green on the left side. There was a pond guarding the left side and Fred had to take his stance with one foot in the water.

Just as he was about to chip it on the green, an exceptionally large crocodile grabbed one of Fred's leg in its jaws and twisted the leg off. Fred fell to the ground screaming and bleeding.

In tremendous pain, Fred looked up at his caddy who was unconcerned. Fred screamed at him, "Why the hell didn't you shoot the fucking thing?"

"I'm sorry, Fred," said the caddy, "This short par 3 is handicap hole 17, and you don't get a shot here."

If you need a free health analysis of your urine, piss under a tree or heavy bushes during your golf round and use these guidelines:

- If you see ants swarm, you have too much sugar.

- If you see flies swarm, you may have an infection.
- If the urine dries up quickly, you have too much salt.
- If you don't remember to lower your underpants, you may have Alzheimer's.
- If you fall while peeing, you're probably drunk, and had too much beer.
- If you pee in your pants you may have Parkinson's.
- If you can't smell the urine, have a Covid test.

Former President Clinton was playing golf with his usual foursome around 9 am on a sunny day. As the day warmed up, he took off his jacket and one of his friends noticed he had panties wrapped around his upper left arm.

Although his friends knew him well, no one questioned why he had women's underwear wrapped around his arm although they were curious.

Finally, as they played more holes, one of his friends had to ask him as the last one in the group finished putting on a green.

"Bill, what's going on with you with the panties wrapped around your left arm?"

"It's a patch...I'm trying to quit."

Joe was a very sly golfer who wanted a certain type of caddy to help him play a golf round with friends. He went over to the caddyshack and asked a small group of caddies, "Which one of you can count and keep a good score?"

A caddy raised his hand and said, “You should pick me, sir, I am an A student in school.”

What's 5 plus 6 plus 5 total?"

"14 sir," said the caddy.

"Excellent! You'll do fine."

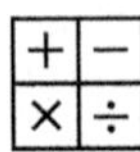

Frank joins a men’s group at a private golf club and the Captain of the club informs him, “You’ll need to give a talk this evening to the other members after golf and since you are a new member, our local fun rule is anyone new in the club has to give us a talk about sex.”

So, that evening, Frank gave a long detailed and funny account of his sex life, and everyone loved it. When Fred got home his wife asked him how it went. Fred was reluctant to tell her he told the men details about his sex life, so he told his wife new members were asked to talk about sailing.

That just didn't sound right to his wife, but she ignored it. The next day, she ran into one of the men who heard Fred's talk last evening and said, "I understand you all heard Fred talk last night. Did you like his talk?"

"Oh, it was great! Fred sure does know what he's doing, and we learned some new things from him."

Fred's wife was puzzled. Then said, "That's very odd, he has only done it twice and got sick during his second time."

One for the 19th hole. A father took his five-year-old son to the local zoo that had the animals in their natural habitat. When they got to the elephants, a large bull elephant was walking through high grass with an erection.

The five-year-old pointed to it and asked, "What's that, Dad?"

"It's his penis, son," said the father.

"I was here with Mom and she said it was nothing?"

"Your mother is spoiled, son."

One for the 19th hole.

His car broke down, so Joe had to take the bus to the golf course. When the bus arrived at his stop, a woman with a baby got off crying.

Hesitating to get on the bus, Joe asked the woman, "What's wrong?"

"That rude bastard bus driver just told me I had the ugliest baby he'd ever seen! Can you imagine anyone would have the nerve to say that!"

Joe said, "Why that son of a bitch, you should go right up there and tell him off – go ahead, I'll hold your doggie for you."

Carl and Carla were just married and having a glass of champagne together after the wedding. Carla says, “Carl, now that we’re married you won't have any time to play golf, so you might just as well sell all of your golf equipment."

Carl replies, "Carla, you sound just like my ex-wife."

"You didn't tell me you were married before!"

"I wasn't."

One for the 19th, Dorothy went to see an old woman with psychic powers. The room was dark and hazy as the psychic peered into a crystal ball, studying it very closely.

The psychic slowly looked up and said, "This reading has some very bad news for you, I'm afraid."

"Just tell me," Dorothy said nervously.

"Alright, there's no easy way to say this, so, Dorothy, I'll just be blunt…prepare yourself to be a widower."

"A widower? Really?"

"Your husband will die a violent, horrible, and excruciating death this year."

Visibly shaken, Dorothy stared at the psychic's lined face, then at the single flickering candle, then down at her quivering old hands.

Dorothy took a few deep breaths trying to compose herself.

Dorothy started to ask the psychic something, then stopped, then realized she simply had to know.

She stared at the crystal ball, then focused on the psychic for several minutes in silence.

Gathering up all her courage, she asked, "Will they catch me?"

Another one for the 19th hole. Dan was an actor for many years and as he aged his memory faded and he suffered from severe forgetfulness and had trouble remembering his lines. He had trouble finding work since most of the casting companies knew he couldn't remember his lines.

Finally, a well-known theater group gave him a chance to act in a role that didn't require remembering a lot of lines.

"Dan, we're going to have you perform one of the most important parts of this play that takes place just at the beginning when the curtain rises. You must walk on stage carrying a rose. Then you hold the rose up proudly with your finger and thumb and smell the rose and your only line is, 'Ah, the sweet scent of my mistress.'"

Dan is excited about being finally given a chance to act again. He buys several roses and practices his part thoroughly and has it down very well.

On opening night, the curtain is about to rise, and he continues repeating the line to himself. Right before it's time for him to go on stage, he continues to practice his one line repeatedly and is totally confident.

The curtain rises and Dan struts on the stage and will great passion and emotion, he says, "Ah, the sweet scent of my mistress."

Suddenly, there were screams of laughter in the crowded theater. The director is going bezerk, "Dan, you idiot! You wrecked this play!"

"But I remembered my line?"

"Yeah, but you forgot the rose!"

"My wife left me for my golfing partner," Ed said.

"Oh, sorry to hear that, Ed. How are you doing and there's plenty of fish in the sea," Mary told him.

"I don't give a hoot about her," Ed said. "I really liked playing with him since he was only one of the very few guys, I could beat golfing."

Carl and Carla rushed to the dentist. Their car came to a screeching halt in front of the office entrance and they raced through the door.

Pushing others out of the way, Carl told the receptionist, "We're in a hell of a hurry! People are waiting for me to join them golfing in a bit and a tooth must be pulled and I don't have time to wait for the anesthetic to kick in! I need the dentist to just yank that tooth out as fast as he can and be done with it!"

"Okay, I'll talk to the dentist," the receptionist said.

The dentist came out and spoke with them. "You are very brave to get a tooth pulled without something to kill the pain. Which tooth is it?"

"Carla, open your mouth, honey, and show him."

An elderly couple was playing a golf course they hadn't played in years. The last time they played this course was at a time when they were in their twenties. There weren't any other golfers playing the course they could see, so they took their time walking the course and reminiscing.

As they played the course, they came across a heavily bushed area where they had sex when they were young, and with devilish smiles, they decided to relive it.

The couple went into the bushes began bonking standing up, then the husband, all at once, started bonking his wife furiously like a sailor on shore leave for the first time in months! They were at it for over thirty minutes, non-stop! Then they both fell to the ground completely exhausted.

“Holy golf balls!” She said. “You hadn’t given it to me like that in 40 years!”

“Forty years ago, that fence wasn’t friggin’ electric!”

A golfer walks into a barbershop and asks for a shave and a shoeshine.

The barber lathers his face and slowly sharpens his large straight edge on a dark leather strap, while a beautiful young woman wearing a very low-cut top bends over in front of him and begins to shine his shoes.

The golfer's eyes bulge out! He can't help glancing at her large quivering breasts as she brushes his shoes.

The golfer starts to laugh and says to the shoeshine girl, “You and I should get a room.”

Completely unfazed, the beautiful young woman says, "My husband wouldn't like that."

The golfer says, “What a waste! Tell your stupid husband you've got to work late, and I'll make it well worth your while.”

Unfazed, the beautiful woman continues to brush his shoes, and without looking up says, "You tell him. He's the one shaving you."

Joe was on holiday in Africa. Going through the African bush, he encountered a young bull elephant with its front leg raised and it was bleeding on the ground.

Approaching carefully, Joe saw a piece of wood stuck in the elephant's foot. Joe patted the elephant's leg and gently pulled the wood out with pliers. The elephant carefully placed its injured foot back on the ground.

The elephant turned to Joe and stared at him for some time. Then the large elephant quietly walked away with a slight limp.

Years later, Joe visited a park zoo. As he approached the elephants, one large elephant turned and came out toward Joe.

When the elephant got to the fence, it stared at Joe for a long time even though other people were standing next to him. The elephant repeatedly lifted one of its front feet off the ground in a pattern.

Remembering the encounter years ago, Joe wondered if this was the same elephant. He thought about it, then bravely climbed over the railing, and made his way toward the elephant.

The elephant trumpeted once more, then slowly wrapped its trunk around one of Joe's legs and slammed him against the railing breaking most of the bones in his body.

Joe remarked in the ambulance; it probably wasn't the same fuckin' elephant.

An international flight from Asia to the US was carrying 198 passengers but the crew, unfortunately, discovered an hour into the flight there were only 40 meals on the plane.

After trying to figure out what to do, the Flight Crew came up with a solution. They advised the passengers, "We apologize to you and we are still trying to figure out how this occurred, but we have only 40 dinners on board, and we need to feed all 198 of you on this flight."

A loud muttering and moaning started amongst the passengers. The chief flight attendant continued to try and quiet everyone down, "Anyone who is kind enough to give up their dinner so someone else could eat, will receive unlimited free alcoholic beverages during the entire duration of the flight."

A second announcement was made two hours later, "If anyone wants to change their mind, we still have 40 dinners available."

Charlie, a successful young pro golfer who traveled a great deal on tour, decided to get married to a wonderful woman and they were deeply in love. He proposed, and she accepted, and they planned a large, beautiful wedding.

At the extravagant wedding ceremony in a huge church, the soft-spoken minister began the ceremony.

As the ceremony progressed, the minister routinely asked if anyone had anything to say or a reason the two should not get married, and to "Speak now, or forever hold your peace."

There was a quick moment of utter silence which was broken like the blade of a pitching wedge striking a rock, when a beautiful young woman carrying a new born baby stood up in the last pew and started walking up the aisle toward the minister.

The baby's cries echoed as the young girl continued to approach the front of the church.

Chaos ensued quickly. The bride threw her flowers in Charlie's face. The groomsmen winked at each other, and the wide-eyed bridesmaids couldn't believe what they were witnessing!

The bride's father got up and took a wild swing at Charlie, then put his arm around his daughter, and took her out of the church.

Charlie couldn't believe what was happening but stood his ground as the young woman and baby approached.

Others in the church got up and began to head for the exits.

The minister said, "My dear woman, why on earth did you come up here? What is your reason?"

The young woman replied, "We can't hear anything way in the back of the church."

A wife was terribly upset because her husband, Joe, neglected her for years, played too much golf, and always came home late. So, she decided to take a stand and leave a note,

"Joe, I've had enough of your neglect and shit, and have left you. Don't bother looking for me, I'm gone."

Suddenly, she heard him coming in, so she scurried and hid under the bed curious to see his reaction.

Joe enters their home. She hears him in the kitchen and then his steps into their bedroom where she's hiding. She sees him walk towards the dresser and pick up the note.

Joe writes something on the note before picking up the phone and then makes a call.

"She's finally gone. Yeah, I know, it is about time! I'm coming to see you, baby! Put on that sexy nightie. I love you and can't wait to see you. We'll do all the stuff you like."

He hangs up the phone, takes his keys, and leaves.

She hears him drive off and in a total rage comes out and snatches the note from the dresser and reads what he wrote,

"I can see your feet. We're out of bread. Be back in five minutes."

"Life is very short, so break your silly egos, forgive quickly, believe slowly, love truly, laugh loudly, and don't avoid things that make you smile."

– Ovilia

Epilogue

We hope you enjoyed this book. We'd like to share a story we were told years ago by a golf pro that happened when he was 19 years old.

He was a gifted golfer and finally qualified for one of the few spots open on a PGA Tour event. He was overjoyed with qualifying and was nervous, of course, as he teed his ball on the first hole with his coach/father on his bag. After doing his pre-shot routine, he hit his first drive out of bounds.

A bit shook but eager to make a good showing, he teed up another ball and hit that OB as well. Then he told me, "It got worse from there on out."

He missed the cut but later went on to an extraordinarily successful golf teaching career.

Playing bad golf can be stressful, embarrassing, and excruciating. If you're playing bad and can't seem to correct it and laughing is the last thing you want to do know that a good laugh does work to get you back on track. It has been proven scientifically to improve your focus and make you think more clearly. This is because bad feelings during terrible golf play change your chemical balance, and your mental game deteriorates.

You know the situation. Your mindset tells you you're going to hit the perfect shot then for some unknown reason you top it, or hit it OB.

To prevent this, I've heard one golfer say he pictures a blue sky with white puffy clouds in his mind before he's ready to swing. Another golfer says he just keeps a single thought of making a nice swing before a shot especially a crucial one.

Regardless of the reason(s) for the bad shot, after the unexpected bad shot happens, and you feel the rage and anguish begin to surface, try thinking of something funny.

Sound silly?

Not really. It's been scientifically proven that laughter helps the body to send oxygen to the tissues. In fact, if you combine laughter with exercise (wave your arms and smile), more oxygen will flow throughout your body.

A research project at the Univ. of Maryland studied the effect of laughter on blood vessels. One test group was shown a comedy movie while the other test group was shown a drama.

The test group that was shown the comedy had normal sized vessels with above average levels of oxygen.

However, it was found that the blood vessels of the test group that watched the dramatic movie were constricted and thereby restricting blood flow causing less oxygen to go throughout your body.

Another study was done in a 2014 Loma Linda University Study that proved laughter produces brain waves like being in a state of meditation.

"It's as if the brain gets a workout....which allows for the subjective feeling states of being able to think more clearly and have

more integrative thoughts," - Dr. Lee Berk, Dr.PH, MPH, the principal investigator of the Loma Linda study.

In other words, a good laugh helps you recover and think more clearly and focus.

Laughter has also been shown to break a state of negativity and is extremely helpful in treating Post Traumatic Stress Disorder.

Okay, but how do you start to laugh after an unexpected and traumatic bad golf shot? Here are three tips. First, smile. You've heard it many times. If you want to be confident, act confidently. Likewise, if you force yourself to smile, happy feelings will follow.

If smiling doesn't work, the second tip is to think of an old joke. Keep the funniest joke you've ever heard in the back of your mind and reflect on it and you may begin to feel better.

Third, if all else fails, think of something positive! For example, say to yourself, "My next shot will be excellent."

The simple passage of time normally makes anger subside and you will eventually feel yourself starting to relax.

Finally, if you must, let the anguish out for a second, and try hard to relax after you do, then force a smile and laugh it off.

Your focus should return, and your golf play will improve.

Keep this pocket-sized book in your bag for a quick laugh (or to share on the 19th or any time). It will help you get back to normal and begin to play better faster when bad shots happen.

All the best to you from TeamGolfwell.com

A Final Message

We hope you enjoyed this book. If you liked it, please take a minute to leave a short review on Amazon or Goodreads. Thank you very much.

TeamGolfwell.com

Printed in Great Britain
by Amazon

56851366R00102